YOU ARE MINE, PORCUPINE

Written by Helen L. Wilbur

Illustrated by Stephanie Fizer Coleman

Just a little porcupup
With lots to learn as you grow up.

Like what to eat and where to hide,

So stick close to your mother's side.

Button eyes, big front teeth,

Thick, soft fur, sharp quills beneath.

But watch for danger as you go,

For porcupines are kind of slow.

The woods are deep and dark.
BEWARE!
They're full of hungry wolves and bear.

So don't forget those long, sharp spines
Protect all wandering porcupines.

Quiet in the morning fog,

Curled up in a hollow log.

Sleeping safely though the day,

Until it's time for porcu-play.

Explore the world when it gets dark,

Munch on clovers, leaves, and bark.

Using claws and padded feet,

Climb where porcu-grown-ups sleep.

Swaying gently in the breeze,

See the world from porcu-trees.

Searching for a sweet fern frond,
Porcupette roams near the pond.

A slip, a stumble—tumbles in.

Don't be frightened;

you can swim.

Lots to see, lots to do.   Porcupette sees something new.

Delicious dandelions and clovers—
Leave Mom's side and wander over.

The trees are dark,
air's cold with frost.

Little porcupette is LOST!

A wolf creeps softly through the night,

His eyes aglow, his teeth shine white.

SNIFF,
SNIFF,

smell danger.

What's the matter?

Stand up straight and start to chatter.

Swing the tail,

thump the ground,

Raise the quills
and twirl around.

A growl,
a howl—

the wolf backs out,

A pack of prickles

in his snout!

Porcu-mom comes to the clearing—
"Is that my little one I'm hearing?

Good for you, you scared the wolf . . . .
You're very brave, and there's the proof."

Before the forest fills with sun,

There's still some time for porcu-fun.

"Let's nibble berries, twigs, and then
We'll snuggle in our cozy den."

"With sweet murmurs, grunts, and cries,

I'll sing you porcu-lullabies.

You'll grow and grow;

you'll be just fine.

You are mine, porcupine."

FUN FACTS ABOUT THE
MIGHTY FINE PORCUPINE

You probably haven't seen many porcupines in the wild. They are nocturnal animals, which means they come out at night to feed and explore. During the day they sleep high in trees or in hollow logs, caves, and other protective places.

Though their Latin name means "quill pig," porcupines aren't pigs; they are rodents—like mice, chipmunks, guinea pigs, and beavers. The big front teeth of rodents grow their whole lives to help them chew through tough plants and bark.

Porcupines are spiny. Mixed in with soft fur are long, sharp quills that protect the porcupine from predators. There are more than 30,000 quills on a porcupine. They detach easily when a porcupine is threatened, and stick into the skin or fur of its adversary.

Porcupines eat bark, pine needles, and all kinds of plants. They love salt, so porcupines often eat unlikely things like wooden canoe paddles (with traces of salt from human sweat) or vehicle tires (covered with salt from winter roads).

Baby porcupines are called *porcupettes*. When they are born, their quills are very soft, but they harden within a day. Porcupines communicate with grunts, clicks, and cries. Their eyesight is poor and they are slow moving, but they have excellent hearing and a superb sense of smell.

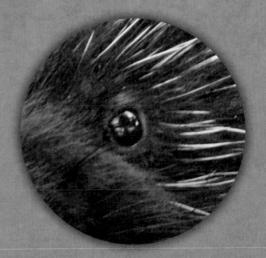

What should you do if you meet a porcupine? Don't try to pet it.

For Marion and Patrick, with love

—Helen

For Mom

—Stephanie

Text Copyright © 2020 Helen L. Wilbur
Illustration Copyright © 2020 Stephanie Fizer Coleman
Design Copyright © 2020 Sleeping Bear Press

SLEEPING BEAR PRESS™

2395 South Huron Parkway, Suite 200
Ann Arbor, MI 48104
www.sleepingbearpress.com

Printed and bound in the United States.

10 9 8 7 6 5 4 3 2 1

Library of Congress Cataloging-in-Publication Data

Names: Wilbur, Helen L., 1948- author. | Coleman, Stephanie Fizer, illustrator.
Title: You are mine, porcupine / written by Helen L. Wilbur ; illustrated
by Stephanie Fizer Coleman.
Description: Ann Arbor, MI : Sleeping Bear Press, [2020] | Audience: Ages 4-8 |
Summary: "A mother porcupine helps her baby explore his world.
Rhyme and witty wordplay take readers through a night in the life of
a young porcupine, relaying facts about its environment, eating habits,
and physical attributes"—Provided by publisher.
Identifiers: LCCN 2019036855 | ISBN 9781534110038 (hardcover)
Subjects: LCSH: Porcupines—Juvenile literature.
Classification: LCC QL737.R652 W55 2020 | DDC 599.35/97—dc23
LC record available at https://lccn.loc.gov/2019036855

Photo Credits: © Nancy Bauer/Shutterstock.com; © A_Lein/Shutterstock.com;
© vanchai/Shutterstock.com; © Jef Wodniack/Shutterstock.com

Grandfather
Twilight

Grandfather Twilight

Barbara Berger

Philomel Books

NEW YORK

Text and illustrations copyright © 1984 by Barbara Berger.
Published by Philomel Books,
a division of The Putnam & Grosset Group,
345 Hudson Street, New York, NY 10014.
Published simultaneously in Canada. All rights reserved.
Sandcastle Books and the Sandcastle logo are trademarks
belonging to the Putnam & Grosset Group
Manufactured in China by South China Printing Co. Limited.

Library of Congress Cataloging in Publication Data
Berger, Barbara,   Grandfather Twilight.
Summary: At the day's end, Grandfather Twilight
walks in the forest to perform his evening task,
bringing the miracle of night to the world.
[1. Twilight—Fiction. 2. Night—Fiction] I. Title.
PZ7.B4513Gr 1984   [Fic]   83-19490
ISBN 0-399-20996-4(hc)
32
PaperStar ISBN 0-698-11394-2

To Dad

Grandfather Twilight lives among the trees.

When day is done, he closes his book,
combs his beard, and puts on his jacket.

Next, he opens a wooden chest that is
filled with an endless strand of pearls.
He lifts the strand, takes one pearl from it,
and closes the chest again.

Then, holding the pearl in his hand,
Grandfather Twilight goes for a walk.

The pearl grows larger with every step.

Leaves begin to whisper. Little birds hush.

Gently, he gives the pearl to the silence
above the sea.

Then Grandfather Twilight

goes home again.

He gets ready for bed.

And he goes to sleep.

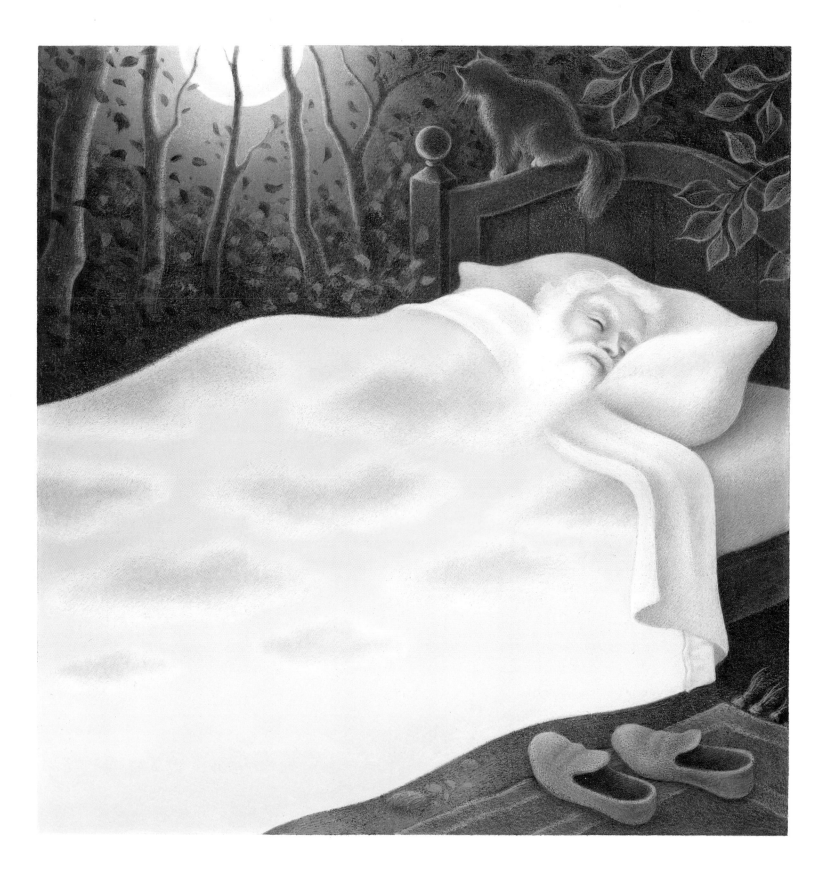

Good night.